MW01601948

My Buddies...

Cuddles to Chaos

1

My Buddies...

Cuddles to Chaos

By Clay Westfall

Publications

Clay Westfall

The characters in this book may seem to be fictitious, but they are our boys. Any similarity to anyone else's family is unintentional and purely coincidental.

©2014 by Robert C. Westfall
Copyright © MMXIV by Robert C. Westfall Publications

Any correspondence can be forwarded to:
www.claywestfall.com

ISBN-13: 978-1499190793
ISBN-10: 1499190794

Dedication

This book is dedicated to
my beautiful wife, Olechka.
She is also the brave mother of
David, Alex and Dmitri.

Forward

When I retired from the United States Navy in 2005, I was very happy. Don't get me wrong, I loved the Navy, but now it was time for me and my wife to take it easy. But, one of the first things you learn when you become a Christian is that God doesn't usually consult with you when He plans your future. A couple months later, we found out that we were pregnant. Now, that is a game changer!

Once our beautiful little David was born, everything was different. Since my career in the Navy had come to an end, it was time for us to concentrate on Olga's career in the Army. With Olga working full time, it was my turn to play the role of stay at home parent. We loved our David very much, and we were blessed beyond belief.

About a year or so later, my wife brought up the idea of adoption. As we looked at our lives, we saw how blessed we were, and decided that we could probably squeeze a couple more chairs under the dining room table. With that, we contacted a well-known Christian adoption organization and started the adoption process.

After a year or better of paperwork and jetlag, we were blessed with two more sons. Dmitri and Alex came to us from Sevastopol, Ukraine, and our lives have not been the same. Dmitri was eight years old, and spoke no English at all. The first couple years were a struggle for him, but soon he was talking up a storm. Alex was two years old, the same age as David. He wasn't really taking at all, so it wasn't as hard for him. Alex and David hit it off, and have been as thick as thieves ever since.

Some of the things that they said and got into were just too funny not to share. Every day, I would post the things that my buddies did on the computer for all of my friends to see. After a year or so I saw how much my friends were enjoying the day to day happenings, so I started compiling it all so that one day I might publish it for the world to see. So please, sit back and enjoy the blessings and the laughs that are my buddies...

Here is David and Alex sitting at their breakfast table. Every morning, you can rest assured they were talking about something, and usually with conflicting opinions.

Chapter One

One of the things I love the most about my buddies is the way they communicate. When Alex and Dmitri first arrived in our home, we bought a small table and chair set for the middle of our kitchen, and that's where they usually ate their breakfast. As mommy and I would get ready for work or whatever else the day held, we would listen in on some of the conversations the boys were having.

Just as a side note, I often refer to the boys as 'the bums'. This is done with love and affection, mostly because they have no jobs and mooch all the time.

01 Sep 09 - David and Alex's breakfast conversation:

David: "I like cereal Alex."

Alex: "No you don't, I do."

David: "No you don't, I do."

Alex: "You like broccoli."

David: "No I don't, you do."

Alex: "No I don't, you do."

David: "You're not my friend."

Alex: "You're a do do."

David: "No, you're a do do."

.... The conversation just went downhill from there.

05 Sep 09 - We have been trying to teach Dmitri how to be a good big brother. This morning he was trying to let David win a race, so he said "David... I am not precipitating..." In all fairness, he was right. I witnessed no precipitating at that time.

06 Sep 09 - While bonding with Alex this morning, he sweetly smiled at me and motioned for me to come closer so he could whisper something to me.... then the bum spit milk in my ear! This kid really needs to go to church today!

15 Sep 09 - Alex told me this morning that he does not want a sister. If any of you were planning on sending us one, please cancel it.

21 Sep 09 - The bums watched 'Blues Clues' this morning and decided they all needed nicknames. Dmitri is pork chop, Alex is Biscuit and David was cornbread, but then he said "No daddy... Corn DOG." I guess you are what you eat.

22 Sep 09 - No school for the bums.... Lucky me. Alex told me this morning "I had a dream last night and Jesus wants you to check the mail." Sometimes he is just too cute..... I'd better go check the mail.....

23 Sep 09 - David is having a bad morning. He is mad because he thinks his grapes have bones. I told him they were "boneless" grapes, and then he accused me of hiding the bones. Does anyone know how much it costs to mail a package weighing 29.5 pounds to Europe?

24 Sep 09 – This morning I went in to wake up Alex. As I touched his shoulder and said "good morning, buddy" he looked at me with wide eyes and yelled "Daddy, I lost my car keys!"

25 Sep 09 - David and Alex breakfast conversation:

David: "Alex, I have more than you do."

Alex: "No you don't."

David: 'Yes I do... look."

Alex: "I see a bug."

David: "No you don't, there's no bug in my bowl."

Alex: "Yes there is."

David: "Be quiet, doo doo."

Alex: "You ate the bug."

David: "DADDY, I ATE A BUG......."

28 Sep 09 - Alex and David's breakfast conversation:

Alex: "The clouds are moving."

David: "No they aren't."

Alex: "Yes they are. It's going to rain."

David: "No its not, the clouds aren't moving."

Alex: "Daddy is it going to rain?"

Dad: "No, I don't think so."

David: "Told you so, do do."

Alex: "Daddy, you're not my friend."

Sigh… Once again, it's lonely at the top.

02 Oct 09 - David and Alex breakfast conversation:

David: "Alex, look at the sky."

Alex: "It's red."

David: "Its pink and orange."

Alex: "Daddy, why is it red?"

Dad: "God painted it for you."

David: "Is God in the sky?"

Dad: "Yes."

Alex: "No He's not, Gods in church."

David: "No, Jesus is in church."

Alex: "No, Gods in church, right Daddy?"

Dad: "Oh my, look what time it is….."

07 Oct 09 - David and Alex breakfast conversation:

Alex: "David, I am bigger than you."

David: "I am bigger too... look at my muscle."

Alex: "That's not a muscle, that's your hand."

David: "No, that's my muscle."

Alex: "I have five muscles."

David: "I have twenty muscles."

Alex: "You're a do do."

David: "Daddy, Alex is not my friend."

Alex: "Daddy, David is a do do..."

09 Oct 09 – David came in from outside and said "Daddy, I'm hungry... can I have a sandwich?" I smiled at him and asked "What kind of sandwich would you like?" He looked thoughtful and said "A blue one."

13 Oct 09 - Alex and David breakfast conversation:

Alex: "You took that toy buffalo from child care."

David: "No I didn't."

Alex: "Yes you did."

David: "Leave me alone Alex."

Alex: "Daddy, David took that buffalo from child care."

Dad: "David, you know you shouldn't take things that aren't yours."

David: "I'm sorry Daddy."

Alex: "God is mad at you David."

David: "No He's not."

Alex: "God doesn't like you."

David: "DADDY... DOES GOD LIKE ME?"

14 Oct 09 – This morning David and Alex were looking at a vegetable activity book. David said "Cucumber begins with C." Alex quickly responded "No, listen... cue,

cue, cucumber. It begins with a Q." David looked up and said "You're smart Alex."

15 Oct 09 - Yesterday David and Alex were both busted for sneaking thousands of dollars in play money to day care. We have no idea what's going on, but we have alerted the imaginary police and expect swift action.

16 Oct 09 - Well, everything was quiet this morning until Alex's backpack said "Meow." A quick look inside showed a small grey kitten and a walkie-talkie. If you add these things to all the money I found yesterday, it's starting to look like a re-run of Law and Order....

19 Oct 09 – Alex and David getting dressed:

David: "Daddy, I don't like these pants."

Dad: "Why?"

David: "No pockets."

Alex: "Daddy, this shirt isn't cool."

Dad: "Yes it is."

Alex: "No it's not."

David: "Can I wear my pajamas?"

Dad: "No, those are for bed."

Alex: "Are we going to bed?"

Dad: "No, we're going to school."

David: "You're going to school?"

Dad: "No, you're going to school."

Alex: "Can Sam (the kitten) go to school?"

Dad: "No, Sam wants to stay here."

Alex: "Sam is not my friend..."

20 Oct 09 – After hearing screaming up stairs this morning, I found David crying and holding his right eye. Apparently Alex wanted to show David how to brush his nose, and David got poked in the eye. I had heard about tooth brush injuries before, but I thought they were only an urban myth....

23 Oct 09 – The bums were playing "Jail" this morning. David had been arrested for lying to the cat (obvious criminal intent), Alex was doing time for making too much noise (the writing was on the wall) and sheriff Dmitri was holding court. David paid a fine of $32 and Alex was sent back to Ukraine. Justice prevails...

1 Nov 09 - David explains why he shouldn't wear socks this morning... "Daddy... its Sunday... look out the window. The sun is here. That means I don't have to wear socks. Can you see the sun daddy?"

2 Nov 09 – David and Alex were playing this morning and Alex asked me "Daddy, do boys dance?" I said "Yes, sometimes." Then David threw his hands in the air and said in a disgusted voice "But they don't go 'Doo Dee dah dah'!"

3 Nov 09 - I was singing 'Bear Necessities' from the movie 'Jungle Book" with Alex and David this morning on the way to day care. I didn't realize that my window was opened. While stopped at a red light, a truckload of workers started laughing at me. I used up my last cool points back in the 90's, so I had to leave them an I.O.U....

My Buddies... Cuddles to Chaos

This was one of few quiet moments. When we lived in New Mexico, there were lots of long drives through the desert. Usually, these guys were asleep long before we got to where we were going.

Chapter Two

One of the things that I found the most heartbreaking about the boys was the first Christmas in the States. Whenever Dmitri or Alex got another present from under the tree, they were so grateful that they would come and hug mommy and daddy. It was so touching.

As the boys grew older and more comfortable talking, that's pretty much all they did... talk. They questioned everything from TV commercials to why we used that brand of toilet paper. One thing is for sure, there was never a dull moment!

My Buddies... Cuddles to Chaos

9 Nov 09 – David wanted water. I gave him some. Alex wanted water. I gave him some. David said I gave Alex more. I didn't. Alex said I gave David more. I didn't. Alex said I'm not his friend. David said I don't love him. Alex is yelling. David is crying. Yep. Its Monday....

29 Jan 10 - FREE TO GOOD HOME - Three year old boy, answers to the name "David," wakes up every morning at 5:00 wanting to play. Serious offers only...

1 Feb 10 - I forgot to buy milk yesterday, and now Alex said that I was no longer his friend. (Sigh) Relationships are so fragile around here....

2 Feb 10 – This morning I am in hot water with Alex (again). I made pork chops for dinner last night, but he wanted "basketti". He may never be my friend again...

3 Feb 10 – I am not a big fan of children this morning. I have not slept past 5 AM in over a week. Perhaps this is a good time for David to visit his uncle George in Africa...

6 Feb 10 - Yesterday at school Alex was asked if he knew his Mommy and Daddies' names. He said "Yes... Clay and Honey". Such a bum...

My Buddies... Cuddles to Chaos

8 Feb 10 - Well, the bums and I went on a nature walk yesterday, and I told them to keep a sharp eye out for forest animals. About three seconds into the walk, David yells "Look guys... a rattle snake." Then, not to be outdone, Alex screams "Look guys, a giraffe!"

9 Feb 10 - Well, Alex and David were eating breakfast. One of the cats jumped onto the table, knocking Alex's cereal in his lap and all over the floor. David tried to move out of the way, knocking his cereal bowl into his lap. Does anyone have any good recipes for fresh cat?

9 Feb 10 - David and Alex and I were wrestling in the living room after dinner. I didn't realize how much fun we were having until I found out that they both wet their pants! I guess that's quality fun...

11 Feb 10 - Ok... five dozen homemade Valentine cookies, check. Seventy 'Ironman' dollar store Valentines, check. Small cheesy Valentine gifts for the teachers check. Ok... we're good. Happy Valentine's Day!

16 Feb 10 - Well, it was a quiet morning here until I asked Alex to turn off a light. Obviously, David wanted to do it, so he jumped Alex and put him in a head lock. Alex bit David's foot (I think that's an illegal move) and then kicked him in the head. These guys are brutal!

18 Feb 10 - Alex is flying around the room in his Superman underwear. He said

"Daddy, I can save my bwudders if they need help." Bwudders to the end...

19 Feb 10 - I told Alex to stop squirming so much while I was dressing him this morning, and he said "But daddy, I'm trying to grow up."

23 Feb 10 - David is 'teaching' Alex to write his name (the blind leading the blind.)

David: "Alex that V is upside-down."

Alex: "That's not a V, it's a Q."

David: "It looks like an R."

Alex: "No, this is an R."

David: "Wait... there isn't an R in David."

Alex: "Is there a Q in David?"

David: "Uhh... yes... no... I forgot."

2 Mar 10 - David made a wonderful discovery... a spy glass in the center of every roll of toilet paper! His only problem was unwrapping them, but one stopped up toilet later, and his problems were solved! He may be looking for a new home soon...

27 Feb 10 - Our son Alex suffers from a rare condition that needs more public support. He has acute kittynakaphobia... the fear of the cats seeing him naked. Please don't judge him.

27 Feb 10 - You know you are blessed when the first words you hear at 5:30 in the morning are "Daddy, I love you. Let's watch Sponge Bob." (David)

My Buddies... Cuddles to Chaos

4 Mar 10 - Lets see... so far Alex is mad at me because I won't give him any "medakashun" (he is no longer sick) and David is mad at me because I won't give him gummy dinosaurs for breakfast. Once again... friendless... (sigh)

6 Mar 10 - David has finally decided what he wants to be when he grows up. A Teenage Mutant Ninja Turtle. I am not sure if that comes with a retirement package...

7 mar 10 - Alex drew a picture for me this morning. It was a beautiful church with trees and flowers, but there were red scribbles everywhere. He told me that the church was on fire. When I asked him why there was fire, he said "So I can see the fire truck, silly."

8 Mar 10 - Dmitri saw Olga throwing away coupons, and then he saw one for some kind of jewelry. He screamed "Mama NO!! I need that coupon." When she asked him why he said "One day I will have a wife and we will need these things"

9 Mar 10 - I was very proud when Alex said "Daddy, when I grow up I want to be a Police Officer" Finally, a mature decision... then he said "or I will be a bird"

10 Mar 10 - This morning, David heard me tell Alex "You are a sweet boy" so he looked at me in shock and said "Daddy, that's what girls say... are you a pretty girl with pig tails"? I think we have created a monster...

11 Mar 10 - The only way to get David and Alex upstairs to brush their teeth every morning is to turn it into a race. I will say "The last one upstairs is a pretty little girl with pig tails", so they take off. I am always the last one, so nobody cries. This morning I said it and David just looked at me and said "Daddy, you are always the little girl, so today I will help you to be the first"... my buddy....

11 Mar 10 - This morning I found myself explaining to David why a Tyrannosaurus Rex must always brush his teeth. That's one conversation I never saw myself having...

12 Mar 10 – I love my kids, I love my kids, I love my kids, I love my kids...

12 Mar 10 - Up at 5:30 this morning (thanks David) watching Handy Manny and doing my Quantitative Reasoning homework. Could Saturday morning be any better?

13 Mar 10 - I have come to realize that all the brilliant minds of the statistical world who developed the Quantitative Reasoning methods probably never tried to do while discussing the 'Chuggington' plot with two four year olds.

14 Mar 10 - Being a Navy guy, I always like to quote Navy movies like 'Top Gun'. Sometimes when the bums ask me for something, I will say "That's a negative Ghostwriter, your pattern is full." This morning Alex asked me if he could go outside, and I said no. Then he looked at me and said "but daddy, my pattern isn't full."

22 Mar 10 - Today is the day of payback. Today, all wrongs will be righted. Today.... At exactly 8:00 this morning, two cats will be cheerfully and promptly dropped off at the flat shoals vets' office to have various parts of their anatomy removed. That will teach them to spray in my closet. Life... is once again in balance. After hearing that the kitties were at the vet, David insisted that we pray for them so they heal. I must admit... I didn't pray very hard.

9 Apr 10 - We try to teach the bums to always respect ladies and to be gentlemen. This morning Alex burped very loudly, then quickly looked around and said "Daddy, I don't have to say 'excuse me' because Mommy isn't here and we are all mans".

Here is David and Alex when they were three. We were living in New Mexico at this time and they had come home from daycare with their Easter bunny ears. Just too cute!

Chapter Three

As the bums were getting older, we started venturing out to more places. One of their favorite things to do was to go to the nearby state park and walk on the nature trail. I would always encourage them to see who could find the most interesting thing to take to school for show and tell. This would always start a contest to see who could find the best treasure, and usually someone found dinosaur bones or spotted a cougar or something.

One funny thing about the park... at the end of the trail there is a rock about the size of a truck. The bums always had to stand on it and flex their muscles.

26 Apr 10 - Yesterday we were hiking on a trail at Panola State Park, and David was fearlessly leading the way. As we came to a fork in the path I said "Hey buddy, go to the right" and he said "Ok, Daddy... this right or that right?"

27 Apr 10 - Alex told me he can't go to school today because he has a 'skeeta bite. He is also very upset because the cat saw him naked again. This is obviously not a good day to be a little boy.

30 Apr 10 - After eating all they could for breakfast, Alex said "Daddy, my stomach is so filled it hurts" then David said "Yes... my feelings are hurt too".

My Buddies... Cuddles to Chaos

1 May 10 - Good morning people. It's Saturday. The wife is sleeping. David is watching a movie. Alex is driving me nuts. Dmitri is grounded. Yep. Its Saturday....

4 May 10 - Well, I am home from the hospital after getting my knee replaced. One bionic implant and seventeen staples later, all is well. Thanks for the prayers! David and Alex have both told me several times that their knees have been hurting, and they have been limping everywhere. Once a bum, always a bum.

12 May 10 - Alex's class made me the sweetest "Get well" card last week, so I made two dozen gummy bear cupcakes for them to eat while I read them a story today. I haven't decided what to read yet... it's between "Horton hears a who" and "War and Peace"....

21 May 10 - David (4 years) led his class saying the Lord's Prayer at parent's night yesterday. He did it perfectly and everyone is talking about him this morning. I told him how proud I was of him and he said "I did it for Jesus!" This is one of those moments parents live for....

22 May 10 - We were sitting at the table after lunch, and Alex (who HATES naps) asked if we could play a game. I said "Ok, listen close... go quietly up the stairs and climb into your own beds. Then pull the cover up over your heads and hide quietly for two hours, then I will come and find you". They actually did this for about 15 minutes, when they finally figured it out that it was a trick. We were laughing so hard...

25 May 10 - Alex told me this morning "Daddy, I don't want to brush my teeth. Can I just go to the Denstist?"

27 May 10 – David and Alex conversation while brushing their teeth:

David: "Alex, I'm a cool boy."

Alex: "No, I'm a cool boy."

David: "I am cooler than you are."

Alex: "No you're not, you're a dummy."

Dad: "Don't call him a dummy. You are both cool boys."

Alex: "Daddy, am I your buddy?"

Dad: "Yes, of course you are."

Alex: "See David? Daddy said you are stupid."

29 May 10 – David walked out of the bathroom this afternoon angrily tugging on his pants and said "Daddy, my pants won't leave my butt alone!"

1 June 10 - Wow, what a morning! Olga is in California this week, and Alex misses her very badly. He woke up crying this morning, insisting the cats are conspiring against him. He refuses to change his shorts because they are trying to see him naked.

2 June 10 - Alex asked me if he could have cake for breakfast this morning. When I said no, he said "But daddy... we are buddies... buddies eat cake, right?"

4 June 10 - The new baby sitter worked out well. When I got home last night, they were all sitting on the couch watching "Godzilla". Life is good. The only problem is that she is VERY pretty, and the boys are all in love with her. David said "Daddy, she's my girlfriend"

5 June 10 - Its tough paying games with Alex. Every time he gets a match, he laughs at me. Every time I get a match, he looks at me with sad eyes and says "Daddy, if you love me, you will give me your match". Then, at the end of the game, he points and laughs at me, and calls me a looser. Fatherhood can be brutal sometimes....

9 June 10 - David came to me after daycare today and said "Daddy, I am in charge and everyone is depending on me". I asked him what he was in charge of and he said "Uhhh... I don't know." I'm thinking a possible career in politics?

29 May 10 – Alex came running into the house this afternoon and yelled "Daddy, there's a raccoon in the yard!" I followed him to where it was and started laughing. "No buddy, that's a cocoon."

14 June 10 - This weekend the bums visited Maxwell AFB in Montgomery, and were looking at all the huge planes and helicopters by the parade field. Alex said with big eyes "Daddy, I want to grow up and fly this helicopter." I said "Good for you Alex. David, what do you want to do?" David said "I really just want to go potty."

15 June 10 - Alex and I were just watching TV and a Victoria Secrets commercial come on. When Alex saw all the ladies in their underwear, he said "Oohhh Daddy, that's so nasty". I would love to be able to have taped that for his 16th birthday!

25 Jun 10 - This morning David walked into the living room with a disgusted look on his face. He was holding one grey sock and started scolding Alex "Why do you always leave your socks in the floor? I am tired of you being a sloppy pig." I guess my work is done.....

5 July 10 - Alex is helping me make fried apples for breakfast. He came to me with a sad face and said "Daddy, I am sorry that you can't play. I will help you make breakfast so you can play later." Now he wants to break the eggs. Looks like they will be scrambled...

16 July 10 - This morning David said "Daddy, when I grow up, I am going to be the President" so I said "That's great... What will you do about the economic situation?" He had a thoughtful look on his face for a minute, and then he said "I will just ask Mommy."

19 July 10 - This morning David kept sticking a marker into his underwear, and it looked like he was trying to scratch himself. I asked him if he was itching, and if I could help him. He looked at me in a disgusted way and said "Daddy, I can't get my sword to stay in its holder."

23 July 10 - Alex wants to take our cats to show and tell. When I told him I didn't think that would be a good idea, he said "But daddy... they are intrust-ching things"

26 July 10 - I think 'Shrek 2' has been a bad influence on David. Much to my shock this morning he told Alex that he had a "Firm pink buttocks." Could you imagine this bum saying that to his teacher?

27 July 10 - Alex told me a joke today... "Daddy, what does a pig put on his sunburn? Oink-ment."

11 Aug 10 - Well, I regret to report that Pre-School is not agreeing with David. This morning he said "Daddy, two days of pre-school is enough. Can I stay with you today? Please?"

13 Aug 10 - Well, David came down stairs this morning and sat down next to me. He said "Daddy, will you put on a cartoon for me?" I told him there was no time for a cartoon, since he had to get dressed for school. He started crying and said "But Daddy... cartoons are for kids and you are going to get into trouble..." (Cartoon police?)

14 Aug 10 - This morning David was yelling at Alex, so I told him to stop. A few minutes later, he was yelling again, so I asked him why. He said "Daddy, we are playing house, and I am pretending to be you".

16 Aug 10 – Today is Alexander's Birthday. After breakfast this morning he came up to me all excited and said "Daddy, I am five years old. This is the oldest that I have ever been in my whole life!"

My Buddies... Cuddles to Chaos

David and Alex have been friends since day one. They argue, fight and scream at each other most of the time, but when the dust settles, they are the best of buddies.

Chapter Four

By this time we had moved to the Atlanta area. The house we moved to was much larger, and Georgia had a lot more snow.

Alex was now in Kindergarten and David was in Pre-K. All three of the boys would catch the bus together not too far from the house. Now, according to David and Alex, the school bus was the coolest thing on the planet. They had always been so jealous of their big brother Dmitri because he would ride the bus and they couldn't. The school bus brought brand new challenges to our mornings.

17 Aug 10 - This morning David told me he wanted to give me a card full of dollars for my birthday. When I asked him where he would get the dollars from, he said "The dollar store, silly!" Why didn't I think of that?

26 Aug 10 - "Daddy, can I have some medicine? My breath hurts" ~ Alexander Westfall, age 5

29 Aug 10 - David has been walking around all weekend with a roll of toilet paper. Every time I tell him to put it back, he (very seriously) tells me that he is a toilet paper worker. After checking The Ladders and Monster.com, I have discovered that there is no such position.

29 Aug 10 – This morning I had to bring Alex into the big church, and he wouldn't stop asking questions. I finally snapped at him and he shook his head and said in a loud voice "Daddy, you can't say 'pain in the butt' in church!"

30 Aug 10 - I have been teaching the bums to respect each other. This morning Alex walked up to me all mad with his hands on his hips and said "Daddy, Dmitri isn't etspecting me!"

1 Sep 10 - Well, let's review the issues of this morning: David was mad at me because his book bag is red instead of green. Dmitri was mad at me because his vitamin tasted bad, and Alex blames me because the moon was not white enough. (Really Alex? The moon?) I am starting to understand why people sometimes put whiskey in their coffee....

My Buddies... Cuddles to Chaos

3 Sep 10 - David at 3:30 in the morning (whispering) "Daddy... since mommy is not here, I will sleep in your bed so you are not afraid" My buddy... always thinking of others :)

6 Sep 10 - I love my kids...I love my kids... I love my kids.... I love my kids...

8 Sep 10 - At the dinner table tonight David said "Daddy... I have a friend named Anya... I am going to marry her". Cool. One down, two to go....

12 Sep 10 - This morning David told me that we can't go to church because Alex's knee hurt. Then he said we can't go to church because Dmitri's shirt was not tucked in. Now he is trying to convince us that there is no church today. I can't wait to find out why he doesn't want to go to church....

13 Sep 10 - While walking to the bus stop this morning, David asked me if President Obama had a book bag. When I told him I wasn't sure, he asked if he could send the President one of his old book bags. I told him I would look into it. What do you think? Spiderman or Power Rangers?

14 Sep 10 – This morning Alex came up to me and said "Daddy, when I grow up I want to be a customer."

15 Sep 10 - Alex had to write the word "Five" for his homework. I told him to write it ten times, but after writing the word twice he came to me and said "Daddy, my teacher said we would get into trouble if we wrote a word more than twice". Hmmm... The school system has gotten a lot tougher over the years.

16 Sep 10 - Alex had to cut out three pictures of something purple for his homework. While we were looking through magazines, David happened to get the JC Penney's mail out. When he turned to the women's underwear section, he and Alex both screamed out "OOooohhh YUCK

17 Sep 10 - When the kids got home from school, they started to fight. I told them if they were good, after dinner they could have a fruit smoothie. David looked at me and shook his head, then he said "Daddy, I don't want a floozy"... his mother will be quite relieved...

18 Sep 10 - The bums have a veggie tales CD that has very old church songs, and they love singing them. Right now Alex is going potty and singing "Swing low... sweet chariot..." This kid is killing me this morning....

21 Sep 10 - This morning David looked up at me and said "Daddy, I don't want to get married... I'm just a kid". It sounds like a reoccurring dream I have....

22 Sep 10 - Alex came home mad today, and said he didn't like a boy in his class. I told him "Jesus tells us that we should be nice to people who are mean to us." Alex looked at me and put his hands on his hips and said "I really don't think Jesus said that!"

24 Sep 10 - I told Dmitri he had to do the dishes. When he complained, I told him I would play him a game of FOO's ball and the looser would do the dishes. It wasn't pretty... Who won you ask? Well now, who is on Facebook? HAHAHAHHAHAHAHA...

25 Sep 10 - David woke up this morning and said "Daddy... I have a secret for you." Then he whispered in my ear "I love you." Ok, maybe we will keep this one.

26 Sep 10 - Fresh peach pancakes! Oh my gosh... you would not believe how good they are! The topics around the Westfall breakfast table? Dmitri - who he will one day marry. David - how big his feet grew overnight. Alex - why Superman would never wear a dress.

26 Sep 10 - Great Service today on forgiveness, Since I live with Alex, I had to tape it so I can watch it over and over and over and over and over...

27 Sep 10 - Last night was a great guy's night. Papa Johns and Transformers... the testosterone was flowing! This morning while brushing his teeth Alex said "Daddy, I'm not Alex... I am a transformer." I am not sure if my dental plan covers transformers....

29 Sep 10 - David and Alex came home from school and both stood up tall, put their hands over their hearts and said the pledge of allegiance. Say what you want about Georgia schools, but I am pretty happy that we are here.

30 Sep 10 - David told me this morning that he was done with school. I can just see his resume' now: Education: 8 weeks pre-kindergarten.

My Buddies... Cuddles to Chaos

2 Oct 10 - Alex just ran through the living room with his pajamas hanging from his head. David was chasing his screaming "Cindy...Cindy.... Stop Cindy..." That's my bums....

4 Oct 10 - After saying his prayers, David asked me if he could be president one day. I said "Sure... what will you do when you are President?" He said "I will tell everyone to do what Barak Obama said." All we need is another buck passer...

5 Oct 10 - There is one window on the school bus that won't stay up. This morning I told Dmitri to make sure if David and Alex sit there, he closes it for them. His eyes opened wide and he said "But daddy, I'm afraid... it's haunted!"

5 Oct 10 - Last night Dmitri told his mother "Mommy, you are so cheap" (she found good deals at the store). This evening he said "Mommy, I am hardly doing my homework."

6 Oct 10 – Today I heard David crying in his room, and when I got there he said that Alex wouldn't share. I said "Alex, you need to learn how to share with your brother." Alex looked at me and said "I know how to share, Daddy, I just don't want too."

7 Oct 10 - Dmitri was being "lectured" by a Police Officer about bad behavior. The Police Officer pointed to a Juvenile detention center and said "Dmitri, that's our kiddie jail". Later, Dmitri started crying and asked Olga "Mommy, why do they have to put the nice cats in jail?"

8 Oct 10 – I just finished fixing two plumbing leaks with David's help. All was going well until he suggested I mix the purple primer with the yellow glue to make green. When I explained why we couldn't do this, he got mad and said I was not his friend. (sigh)... the politics of plumbing....

8 Oct 10 - Took the bums to CiCi's pizza buffet.... We burped... we laughed.... we did not eat salad..... we were men.....

8 Oct 10 – This morning Alex was sick in bed. David came to me and asked "Daddy, why is Alex sick?" I said "You gave him your cold, buddy." He looked at me and shook his head. "No I didn't, I still have it."

When it was time for David and Alex to brush their teeth, it was always an adventure. Alex loved to chew on the toothbrush and suck off the toothpaste, while David made mean faces in the mirror, just like in the picture above.

Chapter Five

Well, the boys were getting bigger and bigger. They started showing interest in everything I did, things like house repairs, or remodeling. The good thing was that they were interested, and they were learning. The bad thing was that every chore I did took about twice as long with the bums tagging along.

Dmitri was also trying to be the best big brother he could be. The only problem was if he didn't know the answers, he would just make something up. I guess ours wasn't the most sophisticated household, but it wasn't boring either.

10 Oct 10 - I was reminded this morning of Dmitri's first experience in America. In the airport bathroom he was washing his hands. When I showed him how to put his hand under the soap dispenser, the soap automatically squirted into his hand. His eyes almost popped out, and then he looked up into the air and yelled "Spacibo" (Russian for thank you).

12 Oct 10 - Yesterday, the regular school bus broke down and a different bus and driver brought the boys home. This morning David started crying and asked me if I could fix his regular bus. I wasn't too sure how to answer him, and then a few minutes later, the regular bus and driver pulled up. David reached up and kissed me saying "Thank you Daddy".

13 Oct 10 - I thought it would take me about an hour to rebuild the railing on my deck, but with David and Alex's help, it only took two hours :) Alex actually nailed my wood clamp to the floor. Not as helpful as one would think...

14 Oct 10 - I just overheard David and Dmitri... (David) "Dmitri, how do you spell Tiger?" (Dmitri) "T-I-G-H-O-R."

15 Oct 10 - I am starting to wish we didn't watch "The Karate Kid" this evening. I just went into the bathroom to check on the teeth being brushed, and I was jumped and karate chopped by Alex and David. I will have to sleep with one eye opened tonight...

16 Oct 10 - Why couldn't I have invented the silly band? Someone else is a millionaire and all I get are bums fighting over them. Stupid rubber bands....

16 Oct 10 - Alex asked me if I knew anyone who was Zasperneeze. You would think so, especially after I spent all those years in Zasperneesia...

17 Oct 10 - I woke up this morning with two pairs of eyes staring at me. Obviously, Alex and David thought that five thirty was a good time to get up.

17 Oct 10 - Ok, its football game time with the bums. The game starts at 4, make your own pizzas, pretzels, soda.... guy time. There will be yelling, there will be cheering, there will be scratching... but there won't be any girls. (Sorry ladies)

18 Oct 10 - FREE TO GOOD HOME - Four year old boy, answers to the name of "David", wakes up EVERY night around three o'clock and wants to play. Will consider swapping for gold fish, if bowl is included.

20 Oct 10 - Well, David woke up at three and won't fall back to sleep. I have fallen asleep about six hundred times, just so he can wake me up again. Now, I will do my homework assignment... at 4:22 in the morning.....

23 Oct 10 - Movie night was alright, I guess. We watched 'Cars' for the six hundred and forty-second time. I think I need to hang out with a taller crowd.

24 Oct 10 - The morning is off to a rough start. The Imagination Movers is a re-run, and David is mad at me, since it is obviously my fault. This is a tough environment...

25 Oct 10 - Beauty has been defined as the face of a child, the morning sunrise, the ocean before the horizon... these things will touch your heart. I challenge you to spend a full weekend with my three sons, and not shed a tear of joy when that beautiful school bus drives down the hill in the morning. Monday.... Beautiful Monday..... (sniff)...

27 Oct 10 - Is it me or does the bums school bus driver get better looking each day?

27 Oct 10 - Alex got off the bus today and said "Daddy... we had a Volcano drill at school today!" Once again, the Georgia public school system goes that extra mile...

29 Oct 10 - This morning David said "Daddy, I want to grow up so I don't have to go to school anymore"... it's funny.... I was thinking that same thing in Finance class last night...

31 Oct 10 - This morning Alex was sitting at the table and he said something smart to me, so without thinking I said called him a 'Smart Aleck'. He started crying, obviously offended and said "Why didn't you say 'Smart David' instead of being mean to me?"

1 Nov 10 - <--- (Doing the Monday morning school bus dance)

2 Nov 10 - Today is the day to cast your vote and make it count. I vote for the age of military enlistment to be dropped down to four years old. They are right... I do feel better now!

2 Nov 10 - The kids saw a dead cat in the road today. Alex asked "Daddy, will that cat be dead for the rest of its life?"

3 Nov 10 - David and I are watching "In Harm's Way", a John Wayne Navy movie. A minute ago he looked up at me and said "Daddy, can I do the Navy when I grow up?" (Sniff)... my buddy...

4 Nov 10 - This morning I was stuck in five lane bumper-to-bumper traffic, when I hear David's voice from the back seat saying "Daddy, if you drive faster we won't be late..." Now why didn't I think of that?

5 Nov 10 - Wow... what a morning! David cried about everything, Alex cried because it was cold outside, and Dmitri didn't brush his teeth due to the cat being in the sink. This family has more issues than Cosmo...

6 Nov 10 - What has six feet, five socks and drives you crazy? Dmitri, Alex and David (who lost one sock). Is it Monday yet?

6 Nov 10 - This afternoon, I was lifting some stones for the patio I'm building, and Alex said "Daddy, you are so strong!" I told him he would be strong when he was older. Then he said "Just wait... when I am 96 years old, I will help you."

7 Nov 10 - The bums were playing in the basement this morning when I heard Dmitri screaming. While lying on his back playing, Alex decided to stomp on his face. I sure hope the sermon is a double feature this morning...

9 Nov 10 - Dmitri and Alex are driving me crazy... They must get that from her side of the family.

One thing the bums like to do is go fishing. Alex and Dmitri are die hard fishermen, but David usually gets bored and will go climb a tree. The problem we have when we go fishing is that the boys will not throw anything back, so no matter how small it is, I have to clean it and cook it. Sometimes, I have to sneak in store bought fish, but that will be our secret.

Chapter Six

One of the coolest things in the world for me is watching World War 2 movies with my buddies. They think everything is cool, and they have learned the names of some very important people, like John Wayne, Sean Connery, and Robert Mitchum.

Members of our family have been in the military for generations. The Army, Navy, Air force and Marines. I would be very proud if any of my sons entered the military, the sooner the better! The least I can do is get them prepared, and what better way to do that then old movies...

12 Nov 10 - David and I are watching a World War II Submarine movie. When I told him I used to be on a Submarine, he said "No, really daddy... what did you do in the Navy?"

14 Nov 10 - Dmitri hardly ever watches regular TV, but this morning I left him watching a wildlife show while I showered. When I came back he ran up to me very excited and said "Daddy... Kroger has the lowest prices in town for all of our Thanksgiving needs!"

15 Nov 10 – A Monday poem...
I love my kids, don't get me wrong,
I'm not that kind of fellow;
But my hero comes on Monday morning,
and his ride is big and yellow.

16 Nov 10 - David asked what was for dinner. I said "Turkey." Alex said "Can I see its head?" I said "No, he doesn't have a head." David asked "What happened to his head?" I said "It got chopped off." Alex asked "Are you mad at him?" When I didn't answer, David asked "Daddy, are you mad at us?"

17 Nov 10 - David was outside riding his bicycle in the cold weather.... wearing the long sleeve shirt, coat, hat and long pants I told him to wear. Then I looked at his feet and saw he was bare-footed wearing flip-flops...

19 Nov 10 – Alex was sitting in the floor looking at toys in a magazine. He tugged at my pants and said "Daddy, I want a bicycle." I answered "from Santa Clause?" Alex said "No, from Walmart."

20 Nov 10 - We have been teaching David and Alex about money. This morning Alex gave me 50 play dollars for two pieces of toast, and David gave me 72 play dollars for a bowl of Count Chocula. They probably won't be managing the check book anytime soon...

1 Dec 10 - Back a few years ago, our team had to coordinate a joint effort in the Persian Gulf. We worked closely with the State Department, the CIA, Interpol, the Saudi Special Forces and the Marine Corps. It took several weeks to put everything into motion, and the White House was watching.... That entire operation was less stressful than decorating this Christmas tree with Alex and David...

2 Dec 10 - I was listening outside of Alex's room while he was playing. He has a race car up to his ear (like a phone) and said "Hello, I just got a call on my pager... the man is dead... by a police car on a dinosaur.... I need 911.... thank you.... what? We are going to the zoo... OK... have a good night..... bye"

3 Dec 10 – David told me a joke today. "Daddy, why was 6 afraid of 7?" I answered "I don't know, buddy. Why was 6 afraid of 7?" Because 7 '8' 9... get it?"

4 Dec 10 - I was teaching the bums to play 20 questions. David thought of a movie person, and I asked questions: "Is it a man or woman? Is it real or cartoon? Do we have this movie?" When it was Alex's turn to ask a question, has asked "David, do you like apples?"

5 Dec 10 - When I was reading the bums a bedtime story, I noticed Alex was holding something. When I asked what it was, he showed me. He had bitten off the heads of two toy police officers, one fireman and one soldier... if this should be my last post... please tell my mother I love her...

7 Dec 10 - David pulled me aside yesterday and whispered "Daddy, your truck is not a truck. It is a Transformer named Tiger Wheels." That might explain why the radio station keeps changing...

11 Dec 10 - I am anxiously awaiting Alex's latest work of art. He said "Daddy, I am drawing a picture of George Washington, Baby Jesus, Barak Obama and God." This should be interesting...

11 Dec 10 - Just got back from lunch with the bums. They like when they can eat with just the guys so we can do guy stuff. I won the burping contest, but Alex said more words while burping. It's a good thing Mom wasn't there... it wasn't pretty.

12 Dec 10 - Home made banana and almond pancakes with strawberry syrup and whipped cream with West Virginia style fried bologna. Now it's time to get the bums in their Sunday best and off to church! Go tell it on the mountain... Jesus Christ is born!!

13 Dec 10 - The kids are on the bus, the bus is going to school; Once again it doesn't rhyme, but who cares? The kids are on the bus and the bus is going to school!!! :)

13 Dec 10 - After an in depth investigation, I found that Alex bit the heads off his toy men because he was experimenting with how strong his teeth (mouth) was. Now that I know the rest of the family is safe, I will remove the garlic cloves from under our pillows...

18 Dec 10 - Alex's teacher gave him some Christmas pencils (6) as a gift. He put them under his pillow (against my advice) and this morning they were gone. So, after a very loud 6 AM screaming match, we discovered Dmitri took them. If I mail a large package to Kiev today, do you think it will get there by Christmas?

19 Dec 10 – David's new joke...
"Daddy, knock knock." I smiled and said "Who's there?" David said "Lettuce." I answered "Lettuce who?" David said "Uh, I forgot."

81

21 Dec 10 - This morning Alex was being bad (I know... shocker) so I told him I would tell Santa. He looked at me horrified and said "Daddy... you know Santa?" I smiled and said "Yep. I talk to him all the time". He shook his head slowly and said "If you love me, you will tell him I'm a good boy".

23 Dec 10 – I woke up this morning and noticed a couple changes with our manger. Obviously, Baby Jesus has some security concerns. The stable was full of soldiers and cowboys, all being led by Spiderman. The good news is, all is secure.

25 Dec 10 - Transformers are like fitted sheets... after a couple minutes of trying to fold them you just wad them up and throw them in the closet...

25 Dec 10 - A white Christmas in Atlanta... and still snowing :)

26 Dec 10 - Alex has a chalk board counter for how many days until Christmas. This morning, he asked how many days to write, so I said "since Christmas was yesterday, there are 364 days." He frowned and said "No daddy. Look out the window. See the snow? I will put five days". Once again, confirmation that he will be a Lawyer when he grows up...

29 Dec 10 - Just got home from the commissary. Note to self.... Never ever ever ever ever ever ever ever ever take all three boys to the commissary again.

30 Dec 10 - Breakfast conversation:

Alex: "I love Christmas."

David: "I love Christmas too."

Dmitri: "It's Jesus Birthday."

Alex: "It's Santa's Birthday too."

David: "Santa is bigger than Jesus, because Jesus is just a baby."

Dmitri: "It's not Santa's birthday because there is no Santa."

Alex: "No Santa? Does baby Jesus bring presents?"

Dmitri: "Yes... No, uh, mommy.... uh...."

31 Dec 10 - An optimist stays up until midnight to see the New Year in. A pessimist stays up to make sure the old year leaves ~

31 Dec 10 - New Year's Resolution: I will try to give up children. Wish me luck...

Happy New Year's - The bums make their own hats and party hard. When the clock strikes midnight (actually eight o'clock) we celebrate with noise makers, mountains of cookies and rivers of orange soda!

Chapter Seven

New Years is always a fun time with the bums. We always start off by making our own silly hats, with lots of glitter and colors. Then, we put the clock in a special place where everyone can watch the approach of the New Year. I would always set the clock back four hours so the kids could welcome in the New Year and still be in bed by nine.

As I watch the boys dancing around, being silly, it's obvious to me that these are going to be the memories that they keep forever, one day to pass on to their children. Happy New Year!

My Buddies... Cuddles to Chaos

1 Jan 11 - Wow, its only 6:45 and I already blew my resolution. Kids. Oh well... Happy New Year everyone!

2 Jan 11 - Alex walked into the main church today (usually he doesn't) and when he saw all the people, he looked around and said "Mommy, where's Jesus?" Mommy touched his chest and said "He's here in your heart." Alex quickly felt his chest and said "Mommy, I can feel His head...."

3 Jan 11 – A New Years Poem...
The New Year's here, the old one's gone,
but my morning is filled with sorrow;
my kids are still here, driving me nuts,
'cause they don't go back till tomorrow.

87

3 Jan 11 - So far this morning I have washed a pee'd bed and helped special agent Oso on two secret missions.... 2011 should be uphill from here on :) Happy Monday folks!

4 Jan 11- *A Tuesday poem...*
A baby born, a sunset watched;
the pitter-patter of a toddler's feet;
I love these things, but they don't compare,
to that bus rolling down the street...

4 Jan 11- I just drank a cup of coffee with no interruptions. I watched the news and actually heard all of it.... I can read the Bible this morning without threatening bodily harm to anyone... I am just so... (sob).... happy..... (sniff).... no..... (sob)... kids......

5 Jan 11 – This morning I was helping David put on his shoes. I looked down and said "David, your shoes are on the wrong feet." He said "No they aren't daddy, these are my feet".

6 Jan 11 - David cried because he wanted to wear the wrong shirt. Alex was crying because he wanted to wear the wrong pants. Dmitri was crying because he couldn't wear jeans.... whoever said you shouldn't drink before 7 AM obviously didn't have kids...

9 Jan 11 - Wow... snow everywhere. Do you realize what this means? No..... school bus....... (sniff)...... just.... not.... fair.......

10 Jan 11 - David wants to play in the neighbor's yard. He said our snow was all used up!

11 Jan 11 - We were out playing in the snow earlier, and I told Alex that if he sees one of our neighbors, to say something nice to them (he forgets to be polite sometimes). Later, he saw one of our neighbors and said "I just love your house."

13 Jan 11 - Yesterday I came across a couple of old cell phones, so I gave them to the bums to play with. While we were eating at Wendy's, Alex suddenly grabs his phone, opens it and says "Girl, stop calling me when I am eating... its rude!"

14 Jan 11 - Boy! A whole extra week spent with the bums. At least the snow should be gone on Monday.... a federal holiday.... when the bums will be out of school.... with me.... again....

15 Jan 11 - Last night's dinner conversation:

Dmitri: "Mom, I will need a cake on Valentine's day for my girlfriend."

Alex: "My girlfriend is prettier than your girlfriend."

Dmitri: "You don't have a girlfriend... what is her name then?"

Alex: (thinking) "Uh... Cinderella."

Dmitri: "What? Cinderella is dead!"

Alex: "No she's not... she's my girlfriend."

(D) "Whatever Alex."

15 Jan 11 - I think letting the bums watch "Peter Pan" last night was a mistake. Now they are trying to fly and jumping of off everything. Perhaps I should call the ER in advance and make a reservation...

16 Jan 11 - Tomorrow.... school.... yes.... (praying) please... no hurricanes... no volcanos... no monsoons.... no continental drift.... just take them to school.... please......

17 Jan 11 – Another Monday poem...
The past three weeks there was no school,
with so much snow and play;
But the birds are singing loudly now,
for the bus took the kids away!
(sobbing) I'm just so happy.....

20 Jan 11 - This morning Alex was mad because he couldn't get his shoes on. When I asked him why, he said "Daddy, my feet grew up!"

21 Jan 11 - Wondering if there is a height requirement for military school...

22 Jan 11 - At the dinner table, for some reason we were playing Sponge Bob trivia. Alex asked Dmitri "Who made Sponge Bob?" Dmitri said "I don't know." Alex said "I think God did." Then David said "No, I watch Sponge Bob all the time and I have never seen God or Jesus on there..."

23 Jan 11 - I overheard Dmitri and Alex talking at breakfast. Alex asked Dmitri what the guns on an airplane were called. Dmitri said "those are air conditioners." When I asked Dmitri what an air conditioner was, he said he didn't know. I am thinking he may not be quite ready for rocket science school just yet...

24 Jan 11 – Another Monday poem...

The bus has rolled, it took the kids,
The weekends been so long;
Now it's me in an empty house,
Just singing my Monday song...

24 Jan 11 - This morning when I woke up Alex for school he looked at me through squinty eyes and said "Can you bring me some coffee?"

28 Jan 11 - Last night when we were praying for Aunt Tammie, David asked what his baby cousin's name was going to be. When I said it didn't have a name yet, he asked if he could name it. I told him no. I mean, unless they want a baby named "Muffasa" or "Shrek" Westfall...

My Buddies... Cuddles to Chaos

29 Jan 11 - Ok, Uncle George... after looking at the picture of the newest Westfall, the bums have come up with suggestions for a name. They are: Moses (2 votes), Alex, David, Dmitri, Daniel, Matthew, and my personal favorite, Peter Pan (that was David... I warned you about him). We love you guys!

30 Jan 11 - This morning Alex woke up crying. He said he was still tired, so I told him he needed to go back and sleep more. "But daddy, I can't." he said crying "I have to start playing." The politics of childhood...

30 Jan 11 - Now Alex is going potty and singing "Oh come, all ye faithful" at the top of his lungs. I honestly spend half of my mornings laughing!

31 Jan 11 - Dmitri's dinner time joke: What is the difference between broccoli and boogers? Kids will eat boogers....
(I know...)

2 Feb 11 - David said he had a dream that mommy and I was being chased by a dog, and he saved us. Alex, not to be out done, said he dreamed about mommy and I being eaten by dinosaurs, but he saved us. No wonder I woke up nervous...

4 Feb 11 - The bums were eating cereal and talking about a dog that was lying dead in the road by our house. Alex said "I wonder what happened to him?" David said "I think a tree fell on him." Mystery solved. :)

5 Feb 11 - Off to Beulah land today. The bums are so excited to see Grandma they woke up before five. Yeah buddy.

6 Feb 11 - I am making 100 wings for me and the bums. The beer and grape soda is cold and the pizza is ready. David and I are rooting for the Steelers, and Dmitri and Alex are cheering for Green Bay. Should be a fun afternoon...

7 Feb 11 - Another Monday poem...
Fun was had at Grandmas house,
The Super bowl has passed;
my bums are on the bus to school,
Thank God, it's quiet at last :)

9 Feb 11 - Yesterday at the dinner table we were talking about Birthdays. Alex made us promise to mail God an invitation to his party.

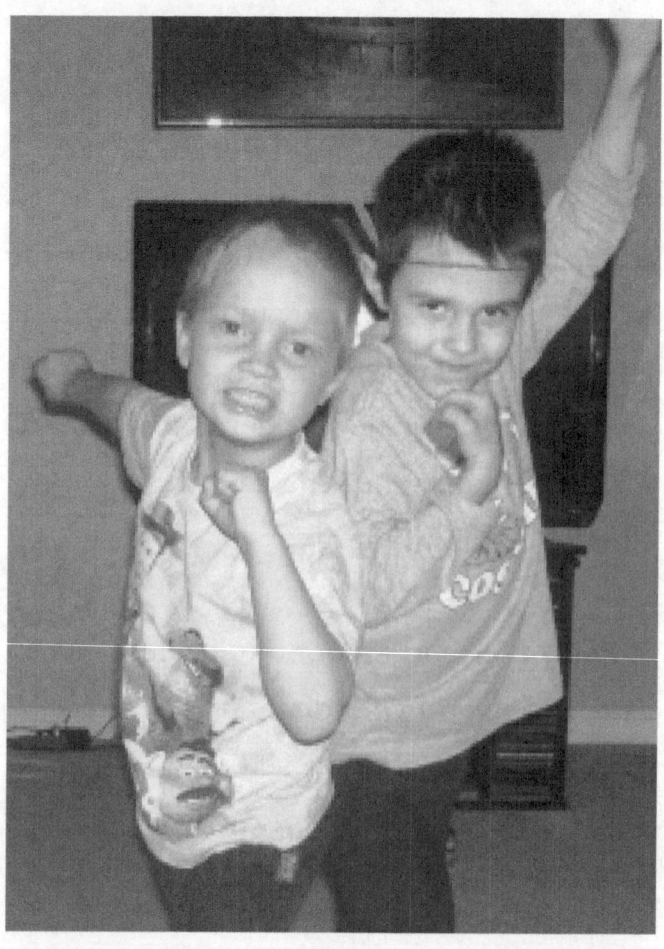

It wasn't too long before the sweet wore off and I started getting attacked from all angles. One super hero movie is all it takes to bring out the tigers!

Chapter Eight

As the boys grew, their personalities really took off. David was always telling jokes (or trying too) and Alex was always running. Dmitri had a hard time keeping up with them, but when he finally did, they were a team.

The picture on the front of this book shows David and Alex in their treehouse. Once they were all in agreement, Dmitri made a sign letting women far and near know that they were not allowed. The boys stayed in that tree house all day, and when we moved to another part of town, they were quite mad that I wouldn't bring it with us.

9 Feb 11 - Alex came home today and told me that his school had another Volcano drill. He was just too cute to correct this time.

14 Feb 11 - What a morning... and at the very last minute, just before the school bus opens its door, David said that magical phrase that every parent loves to hear... "Daddy, I really really have to pee."

15 Feb 11 - Alex usually comes home with two smiley faces if he is good. Yesterday, the smiley face looked a bit odd. That's when we realized he learned something new... forgery. Today its smiley faces. Tomorrow... corporate checks...

17 Feb 11 - David wants to plant a flower garden. I asked him what kind of seeds he wanted and he said "Sun flower" then he thought and said "and rain flower."

18 Feb 11 - This morning Alex asked me what movie we were going to watch tonight during Movie and Pizza night. I said "We are going to see Angela buys a wedding dress." He looked at me with sad eyes and said "But daddy... can't we just watch Transformers again? Please?"

19 Feb 11 - This morning David told me he wanted to be a Pirate when he grows up. I knew sooner or later Alex would drag him into the world of crime...

25 Feb 11 - I have been working on the bums treehouse, and I think it is starting to come together. I proudly showed the bums when they got home to see what they thought and David says "Daddy... this is not right. There is no elevator."

27 Feb 11 - This morning, the bums were watching a movie in the basement, and they heard the song "Viva, Las Vegas." At the breakfast table David started singing the song as he thought it went "Viva, don't spank us."

28 Feb 11 - Rain? Not cool. Alex and David will be very angry with me for not building the roof to the tree house today. They are not as understanding as you might think.

4 Mar 11 - With the new design (don't get me started) on the tree house, I have fallen a bit behind. Yesterday David was in it yelling to me "Daddy, why isn't the roof on yet?" I said I was trying, and then he said "Maybe you should try harder!" Yeap. My buddy...

5 Mar 11 - Someone broke the front window. Alex said it was Dmitri. Dmitri said it was Alex. While they are screaming at each other, David said (with a tear) "It was me daddy. I'm sorry." David is forgiven. Alex and Dmitri are still fighting and blaming each other.

6 Mar 11 - Tonight just before bed David got a light spanking for doing something he shouldn't have. When we were praying he said "Daddy, I love you very much, but you are not my friend."

8 Mar 11 - David is home "sick" today. Last night, Dmitri, while very skillfully demonstrating the ancient art of ninja warfare, stabbed him in the leg with a pencil. David is fine, but was all whining and crying, so I knew the school would call. Dmitri's mail will be forwarded to the military academy he is now attending...

10 Mar 11 - Just before leaving this morning, David runs to me crying and said "Daddy, I don't want my ears to fall off, because blood will run down my shirt!" When I asked him who said that he said "Alex told me not to tell you."

12 Mar 11 - At the Botanical Gardens today, Alex peed (unauthorized) behind a bench. Last week, He peed (also unauthorized) on a tree in Centennial park. Does anyone know the fine for serial peeing in Atlanta?

12 Mar 11 - At dinner tonight Alex said "Mommy, bacon is a meat." Olga told him he was right, and that it came from a pig. Then he looked down at his plate and asked "What animal does chicken come from?"

13 Mar 11 - A couple weeks ago, David and Alex asked me to play music while driving. I stuck in the first CD I saw and an old REO Speed wagon song was playing. Today Alex said "Daddy, play that new song 'Can't find my feelings anymore'..."

18 Mar 11 - Yesterday I saw David walking with a mop. I quietly watched to see what he was doing with it and a couple minutes later he started dancing with it. When he saw me looking he said "Daddy, come and meet my wife."

19 Mar 11 - Heading off to Six Flags with the bums today. Wish me luck.

21 Mar 11 - David fell in the driveway yesterday and scraped his face and elbow pretty bad. Alex is always banged up. This morning David looked at Alex and shook his head saying "Alex, me and you gots issues."

22 Mar 11 - Alex has been bringing books home from school. When I asked him why, he said the library was letting children take some old books home. Just in case, I decided to email his teacher. Today she calls me and said he had been stealing them off the classroom book shelf. I probably need to check him for tattoos too...

24 Mar 11 - What a morning! Alex was crying this morning and asked if he could have a different family. Perhaps he just needs a vacation. Does anybody know how tall you have to be to get on an overseas flight by yourself?

27 Mar 11 - Well, we bought fishing poles today, and a fishing license. Now, if I can only remember how to fish... (We may need Uncle Toby)

28 Mar 11 - I walked in on a conversation before dinner: (Alex) "Spiderman's web can hold anything." (David) "It can't hold God." (Alex) "Yes it can." (David) "No, God is too heavy." (Alex) "Oh, yeah... I forgot."

31 Mar 11 - Alex woke us this morning and said "Daddy, I need surgery on my foots."

2 Apr 11 - Every Saturday, the bums go to a "Soldiers of the Bible" program at church, where they can dress as soldiers. I was telling Alex this morning that I would put on his make up (camouflage) and he said "Daddy, we are man's... we don't wear makeup like girls!"

4 Apr 11 - Spring Holidays... hoo ray. Its 7:25 and these kids are already on my nerves.

5 Apr 11 - I may have broken a record today for the most questions answered in one morning. Everything's from "Daddy, does President Obama play with Lego's" to "Daddy, can an octopus play basketball?"

So far there have been about 652,871 questions.

5 Apr 11 - Well, at least we made it to Tuesday before we had to ride on in to the ER. David fell about five feet head first into the concrete floor of the basement. He had a huge bleeding lump on his head (Alex was quite impressed). Thank God, not too serious. David is now happily bugging the crap out of us as I am typing this :)

6 Apr 11 - I get to take the bums with me to two doctor appointments today! If I make them sit right next to the reception window, they may just rush me right along...

8 Apr 11 - I don't want to say that the kids stressed me out today, but when I (we) were at my second appointment, it was brought to my attention that I not only left the keys in the van, but I left it running in its parking space...

9 Apr 11 - They say a glass of red wine in the evening is really good for you. I must agree! After the kids drank their red wine, they were fast asleep and our evening was quiet and enjoyable :)

9 Apr 11 - Getting the fishing poles ready for tomorrows trip. The bums are so excited, they can't get to sleep. I have been using my fishing expertise to get the gear ready. Let's see... Alex has a green thingy on his, David has a blue dealy and Dmitri's has a three hooky thing. Me, I'll just use my shotgun...

This picture is one of the first ones taken when the boys first came from Ukraine. To this day they all love to wear hats and sunglasses, and often they look like a Hollywood family incognito.

Chapter Nine

At this point in time, the boys were still growing, and they were much quicker about voicing their opinions. The house we lived in at this time was much bigger than the first one, and the bums had the entire basement to play in. They were also starting to get more into sports, and fishing was a regular thing.

Our home has always been a Christian home, and God always found His way into the boys conversations. They would learn new lessons in Bible school, and when they tried to work them into everyday life, it was often quite comical.

10 Apr 11 - Alex had been awake now for about an hour and has already mentioned the fishing trip about 462 times. I think he is excited. He asked me if we could skip church, but when I said no he asked if we could go to church right now.

10 Apr 11 - The bums had a great time fishing. Dmitri didn't catch any. David helped me find worms, and then he adopted one and quit fishing so he could play with it. Alex caught a nice catfish, but as soon as it got to shore, his dad's hook knot slipped and that was that. I could tell from the look I was getting on the way home that Alex was not impressed with my fishing skills. All in all, a good day.

11 Apr 11 - I think that at times like this we must embrace who we are, and just try to hold it together despite our emotions.

It's not easy keeping your composure while trying to look strong. I was strong. I set my emotions aside and I did not kiss the school bus driver this morning...

12 Apr 11 - Last night David pulled me aside and said "Daddy, Alex said something terrible. He said the 'G' word. You have to spank him." When I asked what he said, David said "I will get into trouble if I said it." After granting him full unconditional immunity, David whispered in my ear "He said Goodness Gracious."

13 Apr 11 - Dmitri told me this morning that he has already planned to be rich when he grows up. He also said he will be marrying the prettiest girl in the world. That was easy. Now for the other two...

13 Apr 11 - Dmitri came home and asked if he could brush his teeth. Then he asked if he could take his tooth brush to school tomorrow so he could brush there too. I am starting to think the prettiest girl in the world is in his class...

15 Apr 11 - I finally figured out why the bums fight so much over checking the mailbox. David and Alex were missing, so I found them sitting behind the hedge looking at the JC Penny's swimsuit catalog! Incidentally, they both agreed that the girl with the blue polka dot bikini was the prettiest.

16 Apr 11 - This morning David proved he was management material. As the bums were cleaning up the basement they destroyed, David just walked around did nothing. When Olga told him to pick up a couple toys and put them away, he started crying and said "Mommy! It's not fair! I have the hardest job! You hurt my feelings!"

17 Apr 11 - Yesterday, David threw my shoes in the garage. A couple days ago, Olga put her uniforms in my part of the closet. She already has 99% of the closet. Alex took my English muffin this morning. Is my family trying to erase me? Please... if I stop posting for a few days... ask questions...

17 Apr 11 - As we were leaving the lake today, Alex said "Daddy, we didn't catch any fish." I said "Well, buddy, I am happy just because we could be together." Alex looked at me and shook his head. Then he said "But Daddy, that's dumb." So much for quality time...

18 Apr 11 - Alex wanted to wear shorts today. I told him it was too cold. He threw a fit. I said no. He screamed. I told him to stop. He screamed more. I pushed him out the front door and closed it. He froze his butt off. I let him in. He wore pants to school. Dad 1, Alex 0. Life is good.

21 Apr 11 - At the bus stop this morning, Dmitri was telling his friends how badly he wanted to join the military. He said he wants it more than anything! Then I told him when I was in the Navy and went to Africa, I had to get about 40 shots. After thinking it over, he told his friends how badly he wanted to be a Fireman.

22 Apr 11 - Whoever said the little boys are made of 'snips and snails and puppy dog tails' never got Alex ready for school.

How about 'snakes and fire, and lots of barbed wire'?

28 Apr 11 - Tonight we had Mexican. If you eat Mexican at our house, you have to draw a mustache on your face.

3 May 11 - Mom is out of town, so we had a man's dinner. Hot wings, BBQ wings, Fried wings, and chips and dip. Yes, we also had green beans (with protest). Life is good.

25 May 11 - I told the bums I would take them to lunch today. When they were all in the van, Alex asked where we were going, so I said "Aunt Edna's house o'Broccoli." David started sniffling and said "Daddy, can we just skip lunch?"

9 Aug 11 - I went shopping today... by myself. It was wonderful. I heard a loud noise behind me, and I didn't even care what it was. SCHOOL STARTED TODAY!

16 Aug 11 - Did you know that there are over 7 trillion nerve cells in the human body? How do I know this? Because Alex has been on every last one of them this morning! If that boy says "but daddy, it's my birthday" one more time... it may very well be his last! (whew) Now that I have vented... How is everyone?

19 Aug 11 - Well, tonight is a guy's night with the bums. There will be pizza, wings and soda. We will probably watch Godzilla or Jurassic park. It will be a time for manliness... A time for rude sounds and scratching. There will be no vegetables....

16 Sep 11 - "... so Mr. Westfall, why do you think you would be a candidate for parent of the year?" "Well Bob, after looking for my son David's shoes for over 15 minutes, his brother started laughing and said 'ha ha David... I hid them from you'. After that, I refrained from beating my son Alex senseless and took him to school unscathed."

17 Sep 11 - Alex just came up to me, gave me a hug and said "Daddy, I love you and I am sorry if I am a pain in the butt." Ok, maybe I won't ship him off quite yet...

3 Nov 11 - Last night we were sitting around the table eating wings. David said "Daddy, I need seven thousand dollars for school tomorrow." When I asked him why he needed exactly seven thousand dollars, he said "I have to buy a jump rope for school." (sigh)... I remember when I was a kid you could buy a used jump rope for a couple hundred...

16 Nov 11 - We have reports from various neighbors that Alex has been knocking on doors every afternoon asking for candy. It seems that he is starting a movement to make every day Halloween. Hmmm... I hear there are homes available in Marietta...

2 Jan 12 - We went to the park again this morning and played baseball. This time, I showed Alex that if he isn't careful, he can get tagged out. When walking home, I said "Well, today you didn't score as much. Do you know why?" He looked at me and said "Yes. You were meaner today."

4 Jan 12 - Ok, what has three legs, covered with spots and runs around in circles? Who cares? The kids are at school!!! HAHAHAHAHAHAHAHA...

18 Jan 12 - Sparks flew this morning between Alex and Sammy the cat. The bad blood started a couple years ago when Sammy kept looking at Alex while he was naked. This morning Sammy scratched Alex, and then bit him for good measure. As the tension builds, it's obvious to me that these two can no longer share the same house. (sigh) I will miss you Alex....

19 Jan 12 – Ok, it starting to look like Alex is going to need punishing. I was talking to one of the neighbors this evening about Alex. Not only is he still asking for candy, but now he is asking for extra candy for his brother David, who is sick at home!

My Buddies... Cuddles to Chaos

20 Jan 12 - Last night, Alex asked me if he and David could stay up late. I said "Ok, I will flip a coin: Heads, I win, Tails you lose". After Alex lost the coin toss about twenty times (amazingly) David came in from the bathroom. After one flip he said "Daddy, that's wrong! I want heads and you can have tails!" I think I know now who the brains of this team is...

Alex, dressed for school as his favorite person from Black History Month. Dr. Martin Luther King Jr.

Chapter Ten

As time goes on, the boys grew and grew. Soon, they were starting to get interested in girls, and learning how to do the really cool things that kids do... forgery, smuggling, assault.... Yep. The weekends were long, and exhausting. Don't get me wrong... as I hope you can see by now, I love my boys. But, I would often tear up on Monday mornings when the bus took them off to school.

Venting was what kept me going, and Facebook was where I vented. I am betting that most of my friends never believed it was all really happening.

16 Mar 12 - Alex asked me if he could invite Zoe (pretty 12 year old neighbor girl) over to have pizza and watch a movie. He is cooler at six that I was.... ever. Of course, I said no. Then he invited his buddy Stephanie (7 year old neighbor girl) and they are watching a movie right now. I am so old...

19 May 12 - This morning Dmitri and I were heading to parts unknown, using the GPS. When the GPS started talking, Dmitri asked why it talked when you could just look at it. Encouraging him to use his brain, I said "Well, you think about it and tell me why." After a minute or two of thought, he said "Oh, I know. It's in case you are blind and can't see it."

2 Jun 12 - Yesterday's trip to the Fernbank Museum held a wonderful surprise for little boys everywhere... They had a special exhibit on poop. It was actually very interesting, but I am not so sure Grandma would approve.

30 Aug 12 - This morning the bums were driving me extra crazy, and just before the point of actually body slamming one of them, I said a quiet prayer... "Lord, if only they came with an instruction book." Then I looked down and noticed that I did indeed have a copy of "The Parents guide to raising children" sitting right on my counter... (The Bible)

2 Sep 12 - This morning David came running into the kitchen with a magazine article. He yelled "Daddy, there is a new 'leave it to beaver' movie... Will you buy it for me? I looked at the picture he had seen... an ad from the original show back in the sixties.

7 Oct 12 - David came to me today with a very thoughtful look on his face. He said "Daddy, I will be in the Olympics when I grow up!" I said "Good for you! What event will you be competing in?" He looked very thoughtful and said "Fishing!" Long live the Redneck Olympics!

9 Oct 12 - Alex has been driving me crazy. But, I think I have figured out how we can use his powers for the good of mankind. I am going to send him to Washington!

President: Give me your guns! Alex: No fair! No fair! (repeat 10 times)

My Buddies... Cuddles to Chaos

President: No more money for the military.

Alex: What? Why are you always picking on me??? (repeat 10 times)

President: The rich will pay all the taxes.

Alex: "What did I do?" (repeat 10 times)

President: We will give you money to sit at home and do nothing.

Alex: How come I have to do it and he doesn't? (repeat 10 times)

President: I will just bypass the senate.

Alex: No! You can't do that! It's not fair! (repeat 10 times)

In six months the President will have a nervous breakdown and resign.

16 Oct 12 - Well, today David and Alex were promoted to yellow belt. To you and me, that means they have learned the basic Aikido skills and have moved up to the next level. To David and Alex, it means they are now masters of the Ninja art, and now evil doers of the world must die...

24 Nov 12 - Well, there was a company (Matthews Tree Service) cutting trees in the neighborhood. When they saw the bums watching their every move, the Forman asked if he could take the boys up in the six-story bucket truck! All three boys got a ride up over the roof tops and haven't stopped talking about it since. It's so nice to see that there are still folks in the world who care more about people than the bottom line.

12 Dec 12 - Wow! What a morning. I am not sure if I should seek counseling or drive to Canada. Friends should not let friends have children.

15 Dec 12 - The bums and I are watching DRV recordings of Duck Dynasty. I think it makes them understand their Uncle Toby and Cousin Donnie better.

19 Dec 12 - The bums told me a funny joke this morning: Sheep: "Baa." Lamb: "Moo." Sheep: "We don't say moo. We say baa." Lamb: "Yes, but I'm studying a foreign language."

24 Dec 12 - As I was picking up the house today, I decided to share my morning's events in a creative, Christmas way.

On the first day of Christmas my children gave to me; a sticky substance on the TV.

On the second day of Christmas my children gave to me; two bloody knees and a sticky substance on the TV.

On the third day of Christmas my children gave to me; three broken cups, two bloody knees and a sticky substance on the TV.

On the fourth day of Christmas my children gave to me; four dirty shirts, three broken cups, two bloody knees and a sticky substance on the TV.

On the fifth day of Christmas my children gave to me; five missing socks, four dirty shirts, three broken cups, two bloody knees and a sticky substance on the TV.

On the sixth day of Christmas my children gave to me; six chocolate hand prints, five missing socks; four dirty shirts, three broken cups, two bloody knees and a sticky substance on the TV.

My Buddies... Cuddles to Chaos

On the seventh day of Christmas my children gave to me... seven balled up snot rags, six chocolate hand prints, five missing socks.... four dirty shirts, three broken cups, two bloody knees and a sticky substance on the TV.

On the eighth day of Christmas my children gave to me... eight chewed up pencils, seven balled up snot rags, six chocolate hand prints, five missing socks.... four dirty shirts, three broken cups, two bloody knees and a sticky substance on the TV.

On the ninth day of Christmas my children gave to me... nine headless soldiers, eight chewed up pencils, seven balled up snot rags, six chocolate hand prints, five missing socks.... four dirty

133

shirts, three broken cups, two bloody knees and a sticky substance on the TV.

On the tenth day of Christmas my children gave to me... ten empty juice packs, nine headless soldiers, eight chewed up pencils, seven balled up snot rags, six chocolate hand prints, five missing socks.... four dirty shirts, three broken cups, two bloody knees and a sticky substance on the TV.

On the eleventh day of Christmas my children gave to me... eleven smudged up windows, ten empty juice packs, nine headless soldiers, eight chewed up pencils, seven balled up snot rags, six chocolate hand prints, five missing socks.... four dirty shirts, three broken cups, two bloody knees and a sticky substance on the TV.

My Buddies... Cuddles to Chaos

On the twelfth day of Christmas my children gave to me... twelve globs of toothpaste, eleven smudged up windows, ten empty juice packs, nine headless soldiers, eight chewed up pencils, seven balled up snot rags, six chocolate hand prints, five missing socks.... four dirty shirts, three broken cups, two bloody knees and a sticky substance on the TV.

25 Dec 12 – Merry Christmas everyone! Our Lord and Savior Jesus Christ is born! I woke up to a bit of a surprise this morning... our usual manger set with the holy family, shepherds, kings, angels and sheep had been slightly adjusted to include four dinosaurs, Optimus Prime, six assault police officers, two small teddy bears, Superman, three cowboys and one small submarine. Not quite like the one I grew up with, but... Merry Christmas!

Every Christmas we like to make cookies and decorate them for the neighborhood families. The bums love dressing in their 'Santa Chef' costumes and decorating the cookies with colored frosting and sprinkles. Alex always messes up the first one so he can eat it.

Chapter Eleven

It was always interesting to watch the boys as they developed. Whenever they saw something cool from the car window or something on the television, they would somehow bring it into their lives. Now, we would never let them watch anything without screening it first for improper content, but that didn't stop them from getting into mischief.

When the show "Gator Boys" started coming on, I thought it was a cool guy kind of show that the bums and I could watch together. Little did I know how it would influence our household...

6 Jan 13 - A while ago I found the bums using my last roll of scotch tape to tape the heads on all their dinosaurs. When I showed my displeasure, Alex said "But Daddy... we are the Gator Boys."

7 Feb 13 - Alex and David got their orange belts yesterday. To you and I, this means they are doing well and advancing to more challenging aikido techniques. To David and Alex, this means that the next time I give them a spanking, there could be repercussions...

21 Feb 13 - If Alex loses any more teeth I will have to chew his food for him...

14 March 13 - Last night we got home from church a bit late, so I was trying to get the bums to bed quickly (you don't want to wake up in this house when David doesn't get enough sleep). Anyway, we said our prayers (yes, we pray for all of you) and as I was leaving David said "Daddy, you forgot to say 'don't let the bedbugs bite'." Being a bit impatient, I said "Don't worry buddy, the monsters ate all of the bedbugs." Note to self: If you want David to fall asleep before midnight, don't mention monsters.

16 March 13 - David and Alex decided to open up a rock store. When I suggested they sell the big ones for a quarter, David said "Daddy, that's not how you make money. That one is fifty dollars!" Needless to say, customers were scarce!

24 March 13 - David made up a Rifleman joke this morning... "What do you call a man with a rifle and a cold?" "Mucus McCain."

28 Apr 13 - Alex had the best catch of the day. We caught two big fish and two little ones. There is no catch and release with these guys... I have to scale and cook everything.

6 May 13 - This morning David woke up with silly putty in his hair. I wonder if anyone will notice the bald spot I cut in his head. Lucky for me he can't see it. Ahhhh... Monday....

10 Jun 13 - You know, this parenting thing would be a lot easier if it wasn't for all these darn kids...

27 Jul 13 - Every Sunday night Turner Classic Movies shows silent movies, most of them made between 1915 and 1935. David and Alex have already watched the same Charlie Chaplain movie four times this week, and when I tried to delete it, they begged me to save it for them. The movies are always G rated. I wish my father was here to watch one with them. Whodathunkit?

17 Oct 13 - We went fishing this past weekend. My wife told Alex not to let his fishing stick touch the water. (sigh)

20 Nov 13 – This morning Alex woke up and asked me if he could start drinking coffee. When I asked him why he said that he needed it to focus.

23 Nov 13 - Ahhhh.... A quiet morning. Dmitri, Alex and David found a new TV show to watch... "Rawhide" (Black and white, 1960). Alex said "Daddy, they should have more shows like this for us to watch." I agree. Happy Saturday!

17 Dec 13 – It's that time of year again, when Alex paints two Santa Clause cookies and eats one.

26 Dec 13 - Today the bums played Monopoly for the first time. What we all learned from this experience is that David has no ambition for capitalism, Dmitri should never be allowed near a checkbook, and one day we will all be working for Alexander.

1 Jan 14 - Happy New Year everyone! I hope your year has started out well. The first thing I did this morning (after praying) was to make David a balloon mouse and Elephant. Now, I will admit that I am not very good at making balloon animals, but David was nice and said "Thanks dad, I always wanted a mouse with a laser cannon on his head."

18 Jan 14 - David has a two week assignment studying stars and constellations. Last night we were looking up at the sky and he pointed up and said "Dad, look! That's Orion's Belt! It is THE most important constellation in the sky!" When I asked why it is so important, he answered 'Without Orion's Belt, Orion's pants would fall down."

19 Jan 14 – This morning I was sitting in the living room watching "In Touch with Charles Stanley" before church. When they film the show, they always pan the camera around and show some of the audience. Well, it just so happened that Olga was in the audience that day, and I saw her on the TV. I quickly froze the picture and called the boys in. I said "Look who is on TV!" David points to a man sitting behind his mother and yells "Look Alex... it's Mitt Romney!"

20 Jan 14 - You know, when I look back at my life, I recognize how difficult some of my struggles were, and how the challenges seemed so overwhelming. But some force deep inside of me seemed to emerge and allow me to overcome my obstacles. I wonder now, where this special force is when my son David has his meltdowns at six o'clock each morning and drives me to the brink of insanity... and then as soon as he calms down and starts to put on his coat and walk out the door, Alex says "David, that looks like a girls shirt." and it starts again... CHECK PLEASE!!!!!

The End

My Buddies... Cuddles to Chaos

Blessings, from the Westfall Family

145

Made in the USA
Columbia, SC
18 October 2025